THIS BOOK BELONGS TO

_____

_____

_____

**Well done
you can now recolor
your favorite pictures**

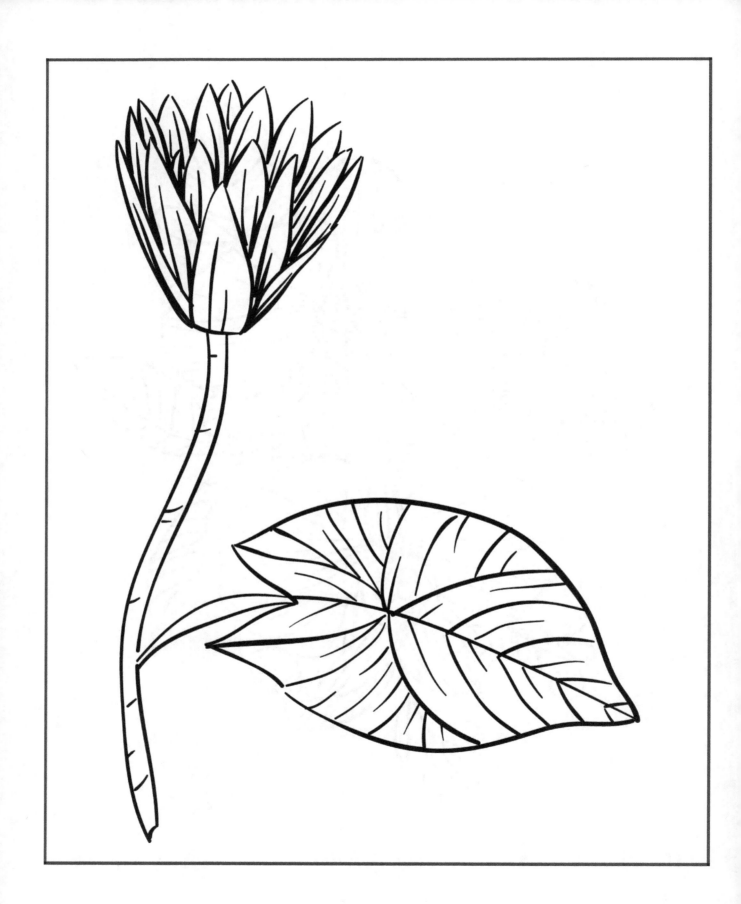

Copyright © 2020

www.ingramcontent.com/pod-product-compliance
Lightning Source LLC
LaVergne TN
LVHW072159150125
801423LV00032B/1252